LIVE IT:
COOPERATION

MARINA COHEN

Crabtree Publishing Company
www.crabtreebooks.com

Author: Marina Cohen
Coordinating editor: Bonnie Dobkin
Publishing plan research and development:
    Sean Charlebois, Reagan Miller
    Crabtree Publishing Company
Editor: Reagan Miller
Proofreader: Crystal Sikkens
Editorial director: Kathy Middleton
Production coordinator: Margaret Salter
Prepress technician: Margaret Salter

Logo design: Samantha Crabtree
Project Manager: Santosh Vasudevan (Q2AMEDIA)
Art Direction: Rahul Dhiman (Q2AMEDIA)
Design: Niyati Gosain (Q2AMEDIA)
Illustrations: Q2AMEDIA
Front Cover: Ryan Hreljac helped raise money to dig clean-
    water wells in Africa. Here, he is standing with his pen
    pal Jimmy from Uganda.
Title Page: Children contribute to Ryan Hreljac's fund to dig
    wells in Africa.

Library and Archives Canada Cataloguing in Publication

Cohen, Marina
    Live it: cooperation / Marina Cohen.

(Crabtree character sketches)
Includes index.
ISBN 978-0-7787-4889-2 (bound).--ISBN 978-0-7787-4922-6 (pbk.)

    1. Cooperativeness--Juvenile literature. 2. Biography--Juvenile literature.
I. Title. II. Title: Cooperation. III. Series: Crabtree character sketches

BJ1533.C74C64 2010   j179'.9   C2009-905524-4

Library of Congress Cataloging-in-Publication Data

Cohen, Marina.
Live it. Cooperation / Marina Cohen.
    p. cm. -- (Crabtree character sketches)
Includes index.
ISBN 978-0-7787-4922-6 (pbk. : alk. paper) -- ISBN 978-0-7787-4889-2
(reinforced library binding : alk. paper)
1. Cooperativeness--Juvenile literature. 2. Conduct of life--Juvenile
literature. I. Title. II. Title: Cooperation. III. Series.

BJ1533.C74C64 2010
179'.9--dc22

05652 4779
7/15

2009036794

Crabtree Publishing Company

www.crabtreebooks.com   1-800-387-7650

Printed in the USA/122009/BG20090930

Published in Canada
Crabtree Publishing
616 Welland Ave.
St. Catharines, ON
L2M 5V6

Published in the United States
Crabtree Publishing
PMB 59051
350 Fifth Avenue, 59th Floor
New York, New York 10118

Published in the United Kingdom
Crabtree Publishing
Maritime House
Basin Road North, Hove
BN41 1WR

Published in Australia
Crabtree Publishing
386 Mt. Alexander Rd.
Ascot Vale (Melbourne)
VIC 3032

CONTENTS

WHAT IS COOPERATION?

COOPERATION MEANS WORKING TOGETHER TO **ACHIEVE** A COMMON GOAL. IT MEANS TEAMWORK, PULLING TOGETHER, AND HELPING EACH OTHER OUT.

THE PEOPLE ON THESE PAGES KNEW THEY COULDN'T ACHIEVE THEIR GOALS ON THEIR OWN, SO THEY COOPERATED WITH OTHERS. TOGETHER, THEY MADE SOME INCREDIBLE THINGS HAPPEN!

ELI MANNING
QUARTERBACK FOR THE NEW YORK GIANTS

TED GROSS AND HIS DAUGHTER NORA
STARTED THE PENNY HARVEST

EUGENE KRANZ
NASA FLIGHT DIRECTOR

HARRIET TUBMAN
"CONDUCTOR" ON THE
UNDERGROUND RAILROAD

RYAN HRELJAC
A BOY WHO BUILT WELLS IN AFRICA

DR. BERNARD KOUCHNER
CO-FOUNDER OF THE ORGANIZATION
"DOCTORS WITHOUT BORDERS"

ELI MANNING

WHO IS HE?
QUARTERBACK FOR THE NEW YORK GIANTS

WHY HIM?
HE NEVER FORGOT HE WAS PART OF A TEAM.

TEAM SPORTS ARE ALL ABOUT COOPERATION. SOME PLAYERS MAY FORGET THIS, BUT NOT ELI MANNING. HE KNOWS THAT WHEN A TEAM WINS, IT'S BECAUSE EVERYBODY WORKED TOGETHER.

FEBRUARY 3, 2008. THE NEW YORK GIANTS WIN SUPER BOWL XLII IN ONE OF THE MOST FAMOUS *UPSETS* IN SUPER BOWL HISTORY.

THAT'S IT FOLKS! THE NEW YORK GIANTS HAVE STOPPED THE PATRIOTS FROM BECOMING THE FIRST *19-0* FOOTBAL TEAM IN NFL HISTORY. AND WORD IS JUST IN THAT THE GIANTS' ELI MANNING HAS WON *MVP*.

GREAT GAME, ELI!

GO GIANTS!

..., HOW DOES IT
..EEL TO BE MVP?

IT FEELS GREAT!
BUT YOU KNOW, I'M JUST
ONE OF 53 PLAYERS. OFFENSE,
DEFENSE, AND **SPECIAL TEAMS**—
WE ALL WORKED TOGETHER TO
MAKE IT HAPPEN.

I MEAN, THINK
BACK ON EVERYTHING
THAT HAPPENED.
THEN YOU'LL KNOW
WHAT I MEAN...

..'S THE START OF THE SECOND HALF.
..HE SCORE IS 7-3, PATRIOTS. THEY'RE
..HINKING THEY'RE ON THEIR WAY TO
..NOTHER VICTORY. BUT THEN...

WE'VE BEEN
ON THE FIELD FOR OVER SEVEN
..MINUTES AND HAVEN'T PUT ANY POINTS
ON THE BOARD! WE JUST CAN'T GET
PAST THE GIANTS' DEFENSE!

OUR DEFENSE
WAS BENDING, BUT NOT BREAKING.
AND ME? I DIDN'T EVEN SET FOOT
ON THE FIELD UNTIL THERE WERE ONLY
6 MINUTES, 43 SECONDS LEFT
ON THE CLOCK. THAT QUARTER
WAS ALL DEFENSE.

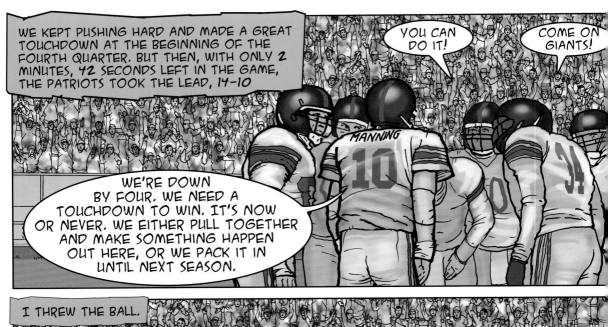

WE KEPT PUSHING HARD AND MADE A GREAT TOUCHDOWN AT THE BEGINNING OF THE FOURTH QUARTER. BUT THEN, WITH ONLY 2 MINUTES, 42 SECONDS LEFT IN THE GAME, THE PATRIOTS TOOK THE LEAD, 14-10

YOU CAN DO IT!

COME ON GIANTS!

WE'RE DOWN BY FOUR. WE NEED A TOUCHDOWN TO WIN. IT'S NOW OR NEVER. WE EITHER PULL TOGETHER AND MAKE SOMETHING HAPPEN OUT HERE, OR WE PACK IT IN UNTIL NEXT SEASON.

I THREW THE BALL.

UNBELIEVABLE! DID YOU SEE THAT? HOW IN THE WORLD DID DAVID TYREE MANAGE TO HANG ONTO THAT BALL? THIS IS DEFINITELY GOING DOWN IN FOOTBALL HISTORY AS "THE CATCH"!

AND THEN, WITH 39 SECONDS LEFT ON THE CLOCK, I THREW A 13-YARD PASS TO PLAXICO BURRESS.

TOUCHDOWN GIANTS!

LIVE

ELI MANNING — SUPERBOWL CHAMPION

SO IT WASN'T JUST ME. WHEN A TEAM WINS, IT'S EVERYBODY—THE WHOLE TEAM, THE COACHES, AND EVEN THE FANS THAT MAKE IT HAPPEN. KINDA LIKE IN LIFE.*

*ACTUAL QUOTE

IT'S EASY TO WANT TO TAKE ALL THE CREDIT WHEN SOMETHING GOOD HAPPENS. BUT ELI MANNING KNEW THAT WITHOUT "THE CATCH" BY DAVID TYREE, THE STRENGTH OF THE DEFENSE, AND THE SUPPORT OF ALL THE PLAYERS, THE GIANTS WOULDN'T HAVE WON.

HOW DO YOU THINK YOU'D REACT IF YOU HAD THE CHANCE TO BE A STAR?

WHAT WOULD YOU DO?

YOU'RE ON A FOUR PERSON RELAY TEAM, AND YOU'RE THE FINAL RUNNER. YOUR THREE TEAMMATES DO A GREAT JOB, BUT WHEN IT'S TIME FOR YOU TO RUN, YOU'RE SLIGHTLY BEHIND THE FIRST TWO RUNNERS. YOU PUT ON A BURST OF SPEED, PULL AHEAD, AND YOUR TEAM WINS. EVERYONE CHEERS AND CALLS YOU A HERO.

WHAT WOULD YOU SAY TO THEM?

TED AND NORA GROSS

WHO ARE THEY?
A FATHER AND DAUGHTER

WHY THEM?
TOGETHER, THEY FOUND A WAY TO HELP THE HOMELESS.

A LITTLE GIRL WANTED TO HELP THOSE IN NEED, BUT DIDN'T KNOW HOW. HER FATHER KNEW HOW TO GET THINGS DONE, BUT DIDN'T ALWAYS THINK ABOUT HIS COMMUNITY. SEE HOW THE TWO OF THEM WORKED TOGETHER TO MAKE A DIFFERENCE.

ON A CHILLY WINTER DAY IN 1991, TED GROSS WAS WALKING IN HIS NEIGHBORHOOD WITH HIS FOUR-YEAR-OLD DAUGHTER NORA.

EXCUSE ME, SIR, CAN YOU SPARE SOME CHANGE?

HERE, HONEY. YOU CAN GIVE THE MAN THIS DOLLAR.

BLESS YOU, DEAR.

WAIT, DADDY. CAN WE TAKE HIM HOME?

THERE ARE A LOT OF PEOPLE WHO NEED HELP, NORA, AND THERE'S JUST TWO OF US. WE CAN'T TAKE THEM ALL HOME.

BUT IT'S SO COLD, AND HE'S SO ALONE.

NORA'S RIGHT. THERE'S GOT TO BE A WAY TO HELP PEOPLE LIKE THIS.

THAT WAS THE BEGINNING OF TED AND NORA'S FIRST PENNY *HARVEST*.

ED DIDN'T FORGET WHAT NORA AD SAID, BUT HE WASN'T SURE HAT TO DO. THEN ONE DAY...

I KNOW I PUT THAT KEY IN HERE. IT MUST BE BURIED UNDER ALL THIS LOOSE CHANGE.

WAIT A MINUTE! THIS GIVES ME AN IDEA!

WHAT? YOU WANT TO KNOW IF I HAVE A JAR OF PENNIES LYING AROUND SOMEWHERE?

YES. AND WHETHER YOU'D BE WILLING TO *DONATE* THOSE PENNIES TO HELP THE HOMELESS.

WHAT A WONDERFUL IDEA! THESE PENNIES AREN'T DOING ANY GOOD IN A BOWL ON MY SHELF!

HURRAY!

11

IN 1994, NORA AND TED WERE INVITED TO BE GUESTS ON THE OPRAH WINFREY SHOW.

...SO MY FRIENDS AND I RAISED MORE THAN ONE *THOUSAND* DOLLARS, JUST BY COLLECTING PENNIES!

THAT'S TRULY INSPIRING, NORA. AND I UNDERSTAND THAT NOW YOU AND YOUR FATHER HAVE STARTED SOMETHING CALLED "THE COMMON CENTS FOUNDATION."

TED AND NORA'S PENNY HARVESTS HAVE RAISED MILLIONS OF DOLLARS SINCE 1991. IN 1997, OPRAH WINFREY BEGAN HER ANGEL NETWORK—AN ORGANIZATION WHERE PEOPLE COOPERATE TO HELP COMMUNITIES AROUND THE WORLD. HER INSPIRATION? TED AND NORA GROSS!

THAT'S RIGHT, OPRAH. WE HAVE KIDS FROM AGES 4-14 DOING PENNY HARVESTS EVERY YEAR. THE MONEY GOES TO ALL KINDS OF COMMUNITY PROJECTS. TOGETHER, WE'RE REALLY MAKING A DIFFERENCE.

IF LITTLE CHILDREN CAN DO THAT, I WONDER WHAT I COULD DO?

WHAT WOULD YOU DO?

A BOY IN YOUR COMMUNITY WAS IN A BAD CAR ACCIDENT. HE AND HIS MOM LIVE ALONE, AND SHE IS HAVING TROUBLE PAYING THE MEDICAL BILLS AND CARING FOR HER SON.

"I FEEL SO BADLY FOR THEM," YOU HEAR ONE OF YOUR TEACHERS SAY. "I WISH THERE WAS SOME WAY TO HELP."

IS THERE? HOW COULD YOU USE THE POWER OF COOPERATION TO HELP THIS FAMILY?

13

COOPERATING IN A CRISIS

EUGENE F. KRANZ

WHO IS HE?
NASA FLIGHT DIRECTOR

WHY HIM?
HE DIRECTED THE MISSION CONTROL TEAM WHOSE TEAMWORK AND COOPERATION SAVED THE CREW OF APOLLO 13.

WHAT HAPPENS WHEN DISASTER STRIKES? THE PEOPLE AT NASA FOUND OUT WHEN AN EXPLOSION LEFT THREE OF ITS ASTRONAUTS TRAPPED **200,000** MILES* ABOVE EARTH.

WITHIN MINUTES, EUGENE KRANZ, DIRECTOR OF MISSION CONTROL, FORMED THE FIFTEEN-PERSON TIGER TEAM. IT'S JOB—TO BRING THE ASTRONAUTS HOME.

*THAT IS ABOUT 322,000 KILOMETERS

ON APRIL 11, 1970 AT 2:13 P.M. THE SPACE SHUTTLE APOLLO 13, ROCKETED INTO ORBIT. ON BOARD WERE ASTRONAUTS JAMES LOVELL, JOHN SWIGERT, AND FRED HAISE.

3... 2... 1... LIFTOFF!

ON APRIL 13, TWO DAYS INTO THEIR MISSION, THE SHUTTLE WAS JOLTED BY AN EXPLOSION.

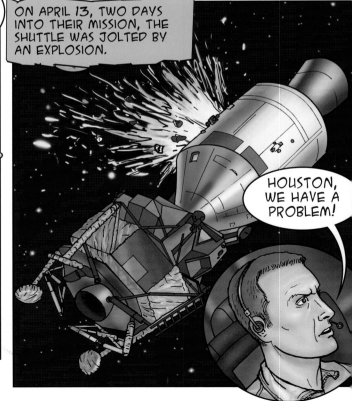

HOUSTON, WE HAVE A PROBLEM!

APOLLO 13 WAS MADE UP OF THREE **MODULES**: THE COMMAND MODULE ODYSSEY; A SERVICE MODULE, AND THE LUNAR MODULE AQUARIUS.

LISTEN UP, FELLAS. ONE OF YOUR OXYGEN TANKS APPEARS EMPTY AND TWO OF YOUR FUEL CELLS ARE DEAD. THE MOON LANDING IS OFF. WE NEED TO GET YOU GUYS HOME.

HOUSTON, ODYSSEY HAS LOST MOST OF ITS OXYGEN. WE HAVE TO HEAD INTO THE LUNAR MODULE. IT IS OUR ONLY HOPE.

THE LUNAR MODULE, AQUARIUS, WAS NOT DAMAGED IN THE BLAST. BUT IT WAS DESIGNED TO SUPPORT TWO PEOPLE FOR FORTY-FIVE HOURS, NOT THREE PEOPLE FOR NINETY HOURS. THE ASTRONAUTS HAVE ONLY A TEN PERCENT CHANCE OF SURVIVING THIS **ILL-FATED** MISSION.

IS DADDY GOING TO MAKE IT HOME?

YES, HONEY. HE'S GOING TO BE OKAY. WE HAVE TO BE POSITIVE.

THE LOVELL HOME, THE NSION WAS UNBEARABLE.

TIME WAS RUNNING OUT. THE CREW WAS SHORT ON WATER, OXYGEN, AND POWER. EUGENE KRANZ KNEW IT WOULD TAKE A TEAM OF PEOPLE WORKING TOGETHER AROUND THE CLOCK TO SOLVE THESE PROBLEMS. HE FORMED THE TIGER TEAM.

THE ODDS OF BRINGING OUR GUYS HOME SAFELY MAY BE SLIM, BUT WE'RE GOING TO BEAT THOSE ODDS. YOU'VE GOT TO BELIEVE, THAT THIS CREW IS COMING HOME. FAILURE IS NOT AN OPTION!*

WE'LL WORK ON WATER!

WE'VE GO POWER!

WE'LL TAKE OXYGEN!

*ACTUAL QUO

SOON, THE TIGER TEAM'S SOLUTIONS STARTED ROLLING IN.

SUIT TEMP CABIN

90 80 70 60 50 40 30 20

IT'S SO COLD.

WE CAN'T FILTER OUT THE CARBON DIOXIDE. THE ODYSSEY'S CARTRIDGES WON'T FIT IN AQUARIUS!

TIGER TEAM HAS SOLVED THAT PROBLEM, TOO! YOU'RE GOING TO MAKE AN ADAPTER WITH A PLASTIC BAG, SOME CARDBOARD, DUCT TAPE, AND A SOCK...

AND IT'S GOING TO GET A LOT COLDER! THE TEAM HAS FIGURED OUT A PLAN TO CONSERVE POWER. YOU NEED TO SHUT DOWN MOST OF THE SYSTEMS THAT USE ELECTRICAL POWER, INCLUDING THE HEATER!

16

ONLY THE ODYSSEY COULD RETURN TO EARTH, BUT THE OLD CHECKLIST TO POWER IT UP WOULDN'T WORK. IT WAS THE MOST DIFFICULT CHALLENGE, BUT THE TIGER TEAM CAME UP WITH A NEW LIST. ON APRIL 17, THE ASTRONAUTS BEGAN THEIR RE-ENTRY.

WE'VE LOST CONTACT.

WILL THE HEAT SHIELD HOLD UP?

ODYSSEY, CAN YOU HEAR ME? COME IN ODYSSEY!

SPLASHDOWN! HOUSTON, WE HAVE SPLASHDOWN!

THEY'RE HOME! WE DID IT! CONGRATULATIONS, EVERYONE!

EUGENE KRANZ, HIS TIGER TEAM, AND THE ASTRONAUTS ABOARD APOLLO 13 ALL RECEIVED THE PRESIDENTIAL MEDAL OF FREEDOM FOR THEIR COOPERATIVE AND HEROIC EFFORTS. THEY SHOWED THAT EVEN IN A CRISIS, COOPERATION CAN HELP PEOPLE ACHIEVE THE IMPOSSIBLE.

WHAT WOULD YOU DO?

HAS A PROBLEM EVER SEEMED SO HUGE THAT IT JUST OVERWHELMED YOU? IMAGINE THAT A TORNADO HAS HIT YOUR TOWN. LUCKILY, MOST OF THE AREA ISN'T BADLY DAMAGED. BUT IN ONE SECTION, HOMES HAVE BEEN DESTROYED, AND PEOPLE ARE WANDERING AROUND IN A DAZE.

HOW COULD YOU AND YOUR NEIGHBORS COOPERATE TO HELP SORT OUT THIS DISASTER? WHERE WOULD YOU BEGIN?

COOPERATING IN THE FACE OF DANGER

HARRIET TUBMAN

WHO IS SHE?
A RUNAWAY SLAVE

WHY HER?
SHE AND MEMBERS OF THE UNDERGROUND RAILROAD WORKED TOGETHER TO HELP THOUSANDS OF SLAVES GET TO FREEDOM.

HARRIET TUBMAN WAS BORN IN MARYLAND AROUND *1820*. SHE WAS FORCED TO WORK WHEN SHE WAS ONLY SIX YEARS OLD.

IN 1849, SHE RAN AWAY TO PENNSYLVANIA. SHE COULD HAVE STAYED THERE SAFELY. INSTEAD, SHE RISKED HER LIFE BY BECOMING PART OF THE UNDERGROUND RAILROAD.

WHILE WORKING IN THE FIELDS ON A PLANTATION, YOUNG HARRIET TUBMAN HEARD STORIES ABOUT OTHER SLAVES THAT HAD TRIED TO RUN AWAY.

I'VE HEARD TELL OF SOME FOLKS WHO ESCAPED TO PENNSYLVANIA. THEY DON'T HAVE SLAVES THERE.

IT'S TOO DANGEROUS. THERE ARE SLAVE CATCHER WITH DOGS THAT'LL HUNT YOU DOWN.

BUT THERE'S FOLKS ALONG THE WAY THAT'LL HELP. THEY CALL THEMSELVES THE UNDERGROUND RAILROAD.

HARRIET WAS DETERMINED TO ESCAPE FROM SLAVERY. ONE NIGHT, SHE MADE HER MOVE AND RAN AWAY FROM THE PLANTATION.

I HAVE THE RIGHT TO TWO THINGS: AND THAT'S *LIBERTY* OR DEATH.. IF I CAN'T HAVE ONE, I'LL HAVE THE OTHER!*

*ACTUAL QUOTE

HARRIET WAS RIGHT.

COME IN QUICKLY BEFORE ANYONE SEES YOU!

YOU MUST BE STARVING. I'VE GOT SOME FOOD FOR YOU AND A CHANGE OF CLOTHES.

SLAVES ON PLANTATIONS ALONG THE WAY ALSO COOPERATED TO HELP OTHER SLAVES REACH FREEDOM.

WADE IN THE WATER, WADE IN THE WATER, CHILDREN...

THEY'RE TELLING US TO LEAVE THE PATH AND MOVE INTO THE RIVER. THERE MUST BE SLAVE CATCHERS AND DOGS NEARBY.

YOU ALL ARE A BUNCH OF RUNAWAYS, AREN'T YOU?

NO SIR. WE GOT OUR FREEDOMS.

I THOUGHT THEY'D CAUGHT US FOR SURE! WHERE DID YOU GET THOSE PASSPORTS?

LIKE I SAID, THERE ARE A LOT OF PEOPLE COOPERATING WITH THE UNDERGROUND RAILROAD. SOME FREED FOLKS IN PHILADELPHIA LENT US THEIR FREEDOMS.

YOU'LL BE SAFE HERE UNTIL YOU CAN MAKE YOUR WAY NORTH TO CANADA.

I CAN'T THANK YOU ENOUGH, AUNT HARRIET! BUT, AREN'T YOU STAYING WITH US?

I CAN'T STAY, NOT YET. THE RAILROAD NEEDS ME. I'M GOING BACK TO HELP MORE PEOPLE FIND FREEDOM.

HARRIET TUBMAN RETURNED TO THE SOUTH A TOTAL OF NINETEEN TIMES. THANKS TO THE DEDICATION OF ALL THE VOLUNTEERS IN THE UNDERGROUND RAILROAD, THOUSANDS OF SLAVES FOUND THEIR FREEDOM—SOME THINK AS MANY AS 100,000!

PEOPLE WORKING TOGETHER CAN ACCOMPLISH AMAZING, HEROIC THINGS. HOW COULD YOU AND YOUR FRIENDS JOIN TOGETHER TO MAKE A DIFFERENCE?

HARRIET TUBMAN and the Underground Railroad

WHAT WOULD YOU DO?

A GANG OF BULLIES IS TERRORIZING YOUR SCHOOL. SOME KIDS HAVE EVEN BEEN BEATEN UP.

"SOMEONE SHOULD DO SOMETHING," SAYS ONE OF YOUR FRIENDS. "SOMEONE SHOULD STAND UP TO THEM."

"RIGHT," SAYS ANOTHER. "AND GET BEATEN UP?"

YOU LISTEN TO THIS, AND WONDER. HOW COULD A LITTLE COOPERATION HELP YOU FIND A SOLUTION?

COOPERATING TO HELP OTHERS

RYAN HRELJAC

WHO IS HE?
A BOY WHO MADE A DIFFERENCE

WHY HIM?
HE *INSPIRED* COOPERATION THAT HELPED PEOPLE HALF A WORLD AWAY.

WHEN RYAN HRELJAC LEARNED THERE WERE PEOPLE IN THE WORLD WITHOUT CLEAN DRINKING WATER, HE DECIDED TO DO SOMETHING ABOUT IT.

IN JANUARY 1998, SIX-YEAR-OLD RYAN HRELJAC WAS SITTING IN HIS FIRST GRADE CLASS.

IF WE'RE THIRSTY, WE CAN JUST GET OURSELVES A GLASS OF WATER. BUT MANY PEOPLE IN THE WORLD AREN'T SO LUCKY.

WHAT DO YOU MEAN, MRS. PREST?

THEY DON'T HAVE ANY WATER NEARBY, RYAN. THEY HAVE TO WALK A LONG WAY AND EVEN THEN THE WATER IS OFTEN DIRTY AND CAN MAKE THEM SICK.

MY NAME IS WALTER. WE DRILL FOR WATER IN EASTERN ONTARIO. OUR *ASSOCIATION* WANTS TO HELP WITH YOUR WELL PROJECT.

RYAN RAISED THE $2000 HE NEEDED. WATERCAN CONTACTED CPAR—CANADIAN PHYSICIANS FOR AID AND RELIEF. TOGETHER WITH RYAN, THEY DECIDED TO DIG THE WELL NEAR A SCHOOL IN UGANDA IN AFRICA.

RYAN'S TEACHER, MRS. PREST, WOULD LIKE OUR STUDENTS TO WRITE LETTERS TO HER STUDENTS. JIMMY YOU WILL BE RYAN'S PEN-PAL.

Dear Jimmy,
My name is Ryan.
I am the well builder

Dear Ryan,
My name is Akana Jimmy.
Our house is made of grass.

Dear Jimmy,
Know what I'm going to do now? I'm going to raise more money so we can buy a power drill and dig a lot more wells.

24

SEVEN-YEAR-OLD RYAN NOW HOPES TO BUY A TRUCK TO TRANSPORT A POWER DRILL FROM VILLAGE TO VILLAGE TO DIG CLEAN-WATER WELLS.

RYAN HRELJAC HAS NEVER STOPPED WORKING TO HELP OTHERS. MORE THAN TEN YEARS LATER, HE STILL HELPS PEOPLE LEARN THAT BY WORKING TOGETHER, THEY CAN DO GREAT THINGS.

YOU DON'T NEED TO BE SOME MULTIMILLIONAIRE. YOU JUST NEED TO DO YOUR PART.*

*ACTUAL QUOTE

RYAN'S EFFORTS LED TO THE CREATION OF THE RYAN'S WELL FOUNDATION. **CONTRIBUTIONS** TO THIS FOUNDATION HAVE HELPED BUILD MORE THAN **500** WATER PROJECTS THAT GIVE ABOUT **620,000** PEOPLE ACCESS TO CLEAN WATER. IT'S AMAZING WHAT A LITTLE COOPERATION CAN ACCOMPLISH.

ARE YOU UP TO A SIMILAR CHALLENGE?

WHAT WOULD YOU DO?

A SCHOOL IN YOUR COMMUNITY HAS BEEN DAMAGED BY A BAD FIRE. ALL OF THE BOOKS AND GYM EQUIPMENT HAVE BEEN DESTROYED. HOW CAN YOU, WITH THE COOPERATION OF PEOPLE IN YOUR COMMUNITY, DO SOMETHING TO HELP?

COOPERATING ACROSS COUNTRIES

BERNARD KOUCHNER

WHO IS HE?
HE IS A POLITICIAN, A **DIPLOMAT**, AND A DOCTOR.

WHY HIM?
BY WORKING WITH OTHER FRENCH DOCTORS AND **JOURNALISTS**, KOUCHNER CO-FOUNDED THE ORGANIZATION DOCTORS WITHOUT BORDERS.

WHILE VOLUNTEERING AS A DOCTOR DURING THE NIGERIAN-BIAFRAN WAR, BERNARD KOUCHNER WITNESSED THE HORRIBLE TREATMENT OF **CIVILIANS**. GOVERNMENTS AND ORGANIZATIONS DIDN'T SEEM TO BE DOING ENOUGH TO HELP. THIS MADE KOUCHNER ANGRY.

HE KNEW HE COULDN'T DO ANYTHING ON HIS OWN, SO HE JOINED FORCES WITH OTHER DOCTORS AND JOURNALISTS. TOGETHER, THEY MADE A DIFFERENCE!

IT'S 1968. THE NIGERIAN WAR IS RAGING. THE STATE OF BIAFRA IS SURROUNDED.

THE DEATH TOLL KEEPS RISING IN NIGERIA. HUNDREDS OF THOUSANDS ARE IN NEED OF MEDICAL ASSISTANCE.

I CAN'T SIT HERE AND DO NOTHING. I'M GOING TO BIAFRA TO HELP!

BUT IT'S GOING TO B[E] DANGEROUS[.]

MAYBE. BUT IT'S EASIER TO BE IN THE FIELD FEELING INVOLVED, THAN IT IS TO BE SITTING AT HOME WATCHING THE WORLD'S **CRISIS** UNFOLD ON TV.*

*ACTUAL QUOTE

SOON, KOUCHNER WAS IN BIAFRA.

THE NIGERIAN GOVERNMENT IS BLOCKING FOOD AND MEDICAL SUPPLIES[.] CHILDREN ARE DYING AND TH[E] REST OF THE WORLD IS LETTING IT HAPPEN!

THE SITUATION BECAME WORSE. IN JUNE, 1969, THE NIGERIAN GOVERNMENT *BANNED* THE RED CROSS FROM PROVIDING AID.

HELP ME! MY SON IS HURT! HE NEEDS A DOCTOR!

THERE'S NOTHING WE CAN DO. THE RED CROSS IS NO LONGER ALLOWED TO WORK HERE.

I DON'T CARE! WE HAVE TO HELP THESE PEOPLE!

WE CAN'T. NOW COME ON.

THIS IS WRONG. EVERYONE SHOULD HAVE THE RIGHT TO FOOD AND MEDICAL ATTENTION, NO MATTER WHAT SIDE OF THE WAR THEY'RE ON!

REMEMBER, YOU'RE NOT ALLOWED TO TALK ABOUT WHAT YOU'VE SEEN. YOU SIGNED AN AGREEMENT.

I'M GOING TO BREAK THAT AGREEMENT! PEOPLE NEED TO KNOW WHAT'S GOING ON. WE ALL NEED TO WORK TOGETHER TO HELP THE VICTIMS OF WAR!

27

RAYMOND, WE NEED A NEW KIND OF ORGANIZATION, ONE THAT HELPS EVERYONE NO MATTER WHAT RACE, RELIGION, OR POLITICAL PARTY THEY BELONG TO! WILL YOU HELP ME?

OF COURSE I WILL.

BUT THERE ARE SO MANY PEOPLE IN SO MANY DIFFERENT COUNTRIES. WE CAN'T POSSIBLY HELP EVERYONE.

IF WE COOPERATE, WE CAN! WE'LL GO TO THE *MEDIA*. WE'LL GET THE WORD OUT. OTHERS WILL JOIN US. YOU'LL SEE!

MY NAME IS DR. MARCEL DELCOURT. I'LL HELP YOU.

I'M DR. MAX RECAMIER. I WANT TO JOIN!

DR. GÉRARD PIGEON

Count me in!

I BELONG TO AN ORGANIZATION CALLED THE EMERGENCY MEDICAL AND SURGICAL INTERVENTIC GROUP. WE'LL ALL WORK WI YOU. TOGETHER, WE CAN MAKE A DIFFERENCE!

WE'LL CALL OURSELVES "DOCTORS WITHOUT BORDERS."

"WE'LL GO ANYWHERE PEOPLE NEED US."

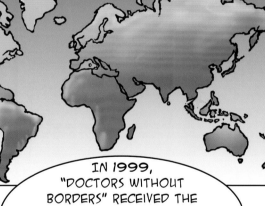

E'LL IGNORE POLITICAL AND RELIGIOUS BOUNDARIES MAKE THE VICTIMS OF WAR OUR PRIORITY!"

IN 1999, "DOCTORS WITHOUT BORDERS" RECEIVED THE NOBEL PEACE PRIZE. TODAY, THE ORGANIZATION CONTINUES ITS WORK, HELPING PEOPLE IN OVER 60 COUNTRIES.

... AND WE'LL SPEAK OUT ABOUT WHAT WE SEE. TOGETHER, WE'LL MAKE A DIFFERENCE.

WHAT WOULD YOU DO?

IMAGINE YOUR CLASS HAS BEEN ASKED TO DO A COMMUNITY SERVICE PROJECT. THE JOB IS HUGE: TO ESTABLISH A FOOD BANK FOR FAMILIES IN NEED. HOW COULD COOPERATION HELP YOU TO ACHIEVE YOUR GOAL?

WEB SITES

ARE YOU INTERESTED IN ORGANIZING YOUR OWN PENNY HARVEST? GO TO THE COMMON CENTS WEB SITE AND FIND OUT HOW YOU CAN GET STARTED!

www.commoncents.org/go/penny-harvest

VISIT THE RYAN'S WELL FOUNDATION WEB SITE AND LEARN MORE ABOUT HOW RYAN HAS CHANGED THE LIVES OF MANY PEOPLE AROUND THE WORLD.

www.ryanswell.ca/

MANY PEOPLE IN OTHER COUNTRIES ARE STILL IN NEED OF MEDICAL HELP. FIND OUT MORE ABOUT HOW DOCTORS WITHOUT BORDERS IS HELPING THEM.

www.doctorswithoutborders.org/

READ MORE ABOUT THE INCREDIBLE RESCUE MISSION OF APOLLO 13 AT THIS NASA SITE.

science.ksc.nasa.gov/history/apollo/apollo-13/apollo-13.html

GLOSSARY

ACHIEVE ACCOMPLISH

ADAPTER A DEVICE THAT MAKES TWO DIFFERENT PIECES OF EQUIPMENT COMPATABLE

ASSOCIATION A FORMAL ORGANIZATION

BANNED FORBIDDEN BY LAW

CARTRIDGE SOMETHING DESIGNED TO BE INSERTED INTO A LARGER PIECE OF EQUIPMENT

CIVILIANS NON-MILITARY PEOPLE

CONDUCTOR A PERSON WHO COLLECTS FARES ON A TRAIN; ALSO, A GUIDE ON THE UNDERGROUND RAILROAD

CONSERVE TO SAVE SOMETHING IN CASE YOU NEED IT LATER

CONTRIBUTIONS A VOLUNTARY GIFT OF EITHER MONEY OR SERVICE

CRISIS AN UNSTABLE CONDITION

DIPLOMAT AN OFFICIAL PERSON WHO DEALS WITH INTERNATIONAL NEGOTIATIONS

DONATE TO GIVE

FREEDOMS OFFICIAL DOCUMENT, LIKE A PASSPORT, DECLARING THAT A FORMER SLAVE WAS FREE

FUGITIVE ACT A CONTROVERSIAL LAW THAT STATED THAT ALL RUNAWAY SLAVES MUST BE RETURNED TO THEIR OWNERS

HARVEST THE GATHERING OF A CROP

ILL-FATED DOOMED

INSPIRED MOTIVATED TO DO SOMETHING

JOURNALIST SOMEONE WHO WRITES FOR A NEWSPAPER OR MAGAZINE

LIBERTY FREEDOM

MEDIA MEANS USED TO DELIVER INFORMATION, SUCH AS NEWSPAPERS, MAGAZINES, TELEVISION, AND RADIO

MODULE A DETACHABLE COMPARTMENT OF A SPACECRAFT

MVP ABBREVIATION FOR MOST VALUABLE PLAYER

PROCEEDS PROFITS

SPECIAL TEAMS PLAYERS ON A FOOTBALL TEAM WHO SPECIALIZE IN RACING DOWN THE FIELD TO TACKLE THE KICKER OR PUNT RETURNER.

UPSET THE UNEXPECTED DEFEAT OF A TEAM EXPECTED TO WIN

INDEX